Impossible Ledges
a memoir in poems

Dianne Avey

A Publication of The Poetry Box®

Editing & Book Design by Shawn Aveningo Sanders.
Cover Photograph & Design by Robert R. Sanders.

ISBN: 978-1-948461-23-8
Printed in the United States of America.

Published by The Poetry Box®, 2019
Beaverton, Oregon
ThePoetryBox.com

For Aidan

Contents

Meeting You For the First Time on the Anderson Island Ferry

You sit on the bench facing me —
wool socks in tan Birkenstocks
opposite my practical black flats —
our toes are the first to meet.

My spine straightens,
leaving its lazy curve
over the book in my lap.
Vertebrae by vertebrae
I am pulled
toward your center,
true north.

I watch,
the tiny cleft in your chin
and the small curve
at the corner of your mouth —
in motion as you speak.

Dappled light,
through a rain speckled window
claims your shoulder,
everything muted and watery,
Monet-like.

I learn,
you are an archeologist.

I wonder,
if you can whittle down
these thin bones of desire

[. . .]

to a fine white dust
that scours across
miles and miles
of my brokenness.

Morning Tide

Our cheeks press toward sunrise
you are weightless above me.

Starfish fingers and rock-crab claws
you pinch, I cling.

Tiny rivulets map us
explorers at low tide,

I turn west to the hollow
of your neck,

tongue dark spelunking
the salty cave above your clavicle.

We ebb and flow
then crash ashore as

desires' undertow releases us
gill-gasping and jelly-fished.

Sleepy sand and sea foam
you moon snail me,

I dream of pearls.

From the Library of Mussels

We are not yet the twisted
branches of old lovers.
We are still drawn
to the scent of lilacs
and the trembling flight
of a hummingbird.

Birch bark curls
up the sides of trees.
Dogwoods open
their white palms to the sky.

In our small boat
you dip oars and
release a nautilus
of sea foam.

You are like the shy plume
that tongues its way
from the barnacle as

you read to me
from the library of mussels,
and feed me the sweet cheek
of a red-red apple.

In our innocence we begin,
not knowing how steep the climb
between sea and sky.
We tell ourselves
this life will last forever.

Immigrants

An explorer emerges
from a secret sea,
slipstreamed into your hands.
His pink lungs expand

as we breathe together,
and count ten tiny
shrimp-like toes.
We linger over
the soft curled pearl of an ear,

as deep currents sweep us
onto this new shore.
Our son's grey-blue eyes—
like mariners' stars—
will be our guide
in this foreign land.

And So It Begins

An ordinary day,
until you reach across
the front seat of our Volkswagen
to hand me
a small white lab slip.

I meet this foe for the first time,
your months of weariness
now has a name—

Leukemia

Our vow—
we will battle this assailant together.
Our weapons, yet unknown:
pills, chemo, radiation,
green tea, vegan diets, acupuncture,
stem cell transplants.

Here on the car deck of our small ferry,
we begin with what armor we possess—
a thin silver breastplate
of prayer.

You don't want to leave
these ordinary days.

Our three year old
asleep in the backseat.

Arriving at Fred Hutch
Cancer Center

You join the army of bald,
bewildered fighters. I join the ranks
of The Tired Ones, those who walk alongside—
holding water bottles, plastic pill organizers,
daily schedules, hand sanitizer.

We learn to be sterile—
politely decline hugs, kiss only on the cheek,
elbow bumps instead of handshakes.
I attempt to explain bacteria to Aidan.

We stay in a small apartment
housing patients and families.
You place plain white mattresses
on the blue carpet, side by side.
You explain you want Aidan close,
you don't want him to be afraid
in this strange place.

Our first week here, a fire alarm
sends us shivering into the street,
someone burned cookies at 2 am.
Chemo keeps no regular hours.

Firemen arrive as
our collective breath rises
under Seattle streetlights.
A huddled mass of hope
wrapped in yellow quilts.

Collapse

Six months later, returning home,
leukemia *cured*, but

        you are dying.

Graft vs. host disease—
our new nemesis.

Tiny moths of antibodies eat away at you,
your vertebrae crumble one by one,
like a stack of Saltines.
I watch
        you diminish.

Once-sturdy cloth becoming threadbare,
light filters through you now.

Your eyes rim with silver tears
as you watch Aidan stack Legos,
building tall towers
of red and blue.

She Who Shows Up

for Vicki

To guide tiny fingers
toward ripening blackberries
and the spiral
of a moon snail shell,

late summer offerings.

She who shows up
with tea and bread,
all the time in the world
to walk hand in small hand.

Our son, beautifully distracted

from the work in the sunroom,
where his father lies
amongst white linen, soft voices,
and falling tears.

She who shows up, and
I remember—
one can still hear
the whole ocean

inside a shell.

Boundary Waters

All that is left for us now—
the silent opening
of dogwood blossoms
pure notes of upturned white,

music from the spilling creek
as it finds its way back to sea,

a distant tap of woodpecker
busy on the last bits of decaying cedar,

the rhythmic rush of wings
announcing winter's first geese.

These last sweet words I cannot speak—
they dissolve into color and light.
We both know the boundary waters
are calling your name.

Mist rises one last time
before it surrenders back to earth.
No need for words, love.
I will kiss you goodbye
for the rest of my days.

In the End

death is rarely pretty.
Maybe it's God's way
of helping us

let go.

I stand watch,
all the while
silently wishing it was over.

Waiting
in our sunroom
filled with morning light,

unaware
of the coming
long days of wandering,

my search to find you again
will take me through
a deep and twisted
thicket of time.

The Morning After You Died

This morning, they came
and took the bed away.

Left behind are a few traces:
syringes, a yellow notepad—
with the neatly checked-off schedule
of morphine, a crayon drawing from Aidan—
one large and one small stick figure
holding hands, looking out toward a rainbow,
a pile of white sheets on the tile floor—
still damp with sweat and urine, and
a few dots of blood.

Evidence.
That you did live, and
you did die, here
in our home.

I begin picking up.
Like the beach after a tsunami,
all those once important items,
now floating around uselessly.

So this is what it feels like
to be on the other side.

I don't know how
to start this life again.

Angle

Bare feet on cool kitchen tile,
a sharp angle of morning light
illuminates once-invisible
dust motes.

Half-formed on my lips, my usual question,
Can I bring you some coffee?
before I remember.

Silence –
   a deafening reply.

I don't ask for healing.
I ask –
   Where are you?

Maybe you *are* here, and
maybe I will see you again,
in just the perfect
slant of light.

Voyager

I hold hands I cannot grasp, lips
I won't kiss again. A hipbone, a rib?
The dull weight of it all. *You.*
You journeyed through
hot white fire, back into my hands.
Your body never as white as these
bits of bone, teeth, ash.
But this is *not you.*

My fingers peel back the lid,
a gritty white ghost in a plain tan box.
The absurdity of an archeologist becoming artifact.
I carry you from room to room,
wondering where to place you?
If I trip, would I vacuum, or even worse – mop,
sending sacred bits of you swirling down the drain?

Later, I drop handfuls of you into the sea.
Mouths of mollusks and silver minnows
will never appreciate the pleasures you gave.
I save a small portion of you.

A tiny wooden box nestles
deep in my lingerie drawer.
There in the dark, I imagine
bits of white knitting themselves
back into your smile,
your teeth beaming like stars
against the black silk and lace.

Impossible Ledges

Black crow pecks at my ankles all day,
tap, tap, tap—Poe's Raven?
Envoy of grief, unwelcome ambassador
of your death. Obsidian beak
tearing away bits of my flesh,
I'm weary of this visitor.

Driving home, I can barely stand
the beat of the windshield wipers,
thud-screech-thud-screech.

I decide to take the long way home,
through slick city streets where tight roads
hem me in with distraction. But even here,
the raven scavenges its evening meal.
Pestering delicate sparrows
who nest on impossible ledges,
and tramples soft ferns that find their way
through crevices in the night sidewalks.

Maybe tomorrow I'll drive home past
the wide-open field, braving the marsh filled
with late autumn light. Where rosehips hang
like ruby baubles, and the air is clear, waiting
for me to stop, long enough to remember
that elusive full breath –
the kind that goes all the way
down to my belly. The breath I haven't known
since you left.

Yes, tomorrow I'll stop there, sit on the bank,
dangle my bruised ankles in the cool water.

There, where the red tail spirals high,
the heron waits, and
even the crows are silent.

Crevasse

It first appears as a tiny crack,
the opening into suffering.
If I am brave, I fall through without grabbing
for my usual handholds of distraction —
laundry, red wine, pity.

What happened
to the small cleft of your chin,
the shape of your mouth,
and landscape of your shoulders?

Where do these remnants go,
the silt of love?

Free-falling down, down, down
to the depths of losing everything
that is you, was you, might have been — you.

At the bottom, I look up.
You lean over the edge, smile, and call to me,
What the hell are you doing all the way down there?

A Certain Sadness

I almost pray for rain today.
A day in which I can sit still,
watch from inside,
away from the distraction
that dishonors this kind of sadness.

Yes, this is just for me,
no one else need bother.
I will wrap it around me
like my grandmother's quilt,

the one tied with bits of blue yarn,
the one I slept beneath for hours,
feeling only the certain weight of stars
in an uncertain life.

Small Deaths

Just a few small deaths today,
the big one has come and gone.
Not the news it once was, people have lives.
No, these ones only I will honor.

Absent, the shuffle of your wool slippers
on their way to morning coffee.
Gone too, the scent of your skin
on your favorite feather pillow.

I miss your glasses
resting atop the latest history novel
on our bedside stand. I even mourn your habit
of leaving your socks on the bathroom floor.

The small deaths of our ordinary conversation
about the escapades of deer in the garden,
the theme of our son's next birthday party,
a dripping kitchen faucet.

Fragments come back to me piece by piece,
moment by moment—a sock here,
a coffee cup there, a touch, a scent—
Today, I will make my way
amongst these small and lovely headstones.

Tomorrow

I will remember what your skin smelled like
when I finally get around to washing
the last remnants of your clothing.

I will place them carefully into white plastic bags,
put them in the backseat of our jeep,
take the ferry across the sound.

Red and yellow Ralph Lauren button-down
shirts and worn blue Levi's, my passengers—
they will speak to me during the crossing.

Tomorrow, I will listen to these garments tell me
how they too, caressed and held you
for all those days, weeks and years.

Smug buttons, zippers with their lips pursed, sleeves with
    arms crossed.
Don't think you're the only one who misses him...we loved him, too
they scold me.

Tomorrow, I will cry watching our six-year-old get dressed
    for school—
small fingers tug a reluctant zipper on a bright yellow jacket,
and blue-jeans, worn through at the knees.

Untethered

Suffocating sorrow,
I plead with the night around me,
a prayer of fists—

Where are you?

Then it happens.

Pulled by some invisible force,
shot like a bolt of electricity,
I ascend, free
from that darkest of nights.

I open—
infinite, unending—
one drop becomes
the entire ocean.

Intersecting golden strands of light,
perfect geometric symmetry.
Timeless music of violins moves through me,
I am the music, I am the light,

In the midst of this relentless love,
I have found you.

I want to stay here forever, but it is not yet my time.
I return, gasping for air, my heart pounding.
Aidan sleeps soundly beside me,
his forehead, moist with dreaming.

Tonight, stars still revolve,
beetles silently work the earth,

[. . .]

and the tide slips in unhurriedly in the dark.

Tomorrow morning,
the cherry tree outside the kitchen window—
the one friends planted two weeks after you died—
will scatter a confetti of white blossoms,
in celebration of answered prayer.

Pancakes

How do I
make pancakes
after going to *heaven*
and back again?
Here in the morning light
of my kitchen,
bare feet on cool tile.

The answer:
with reverence,
astonishment
and praise.

Death, you have lost—
      gone is your sting.

No more will I breathe
that heavy alabaster wind,
cold and unwavering,
my chest once encased
a marble lung.

I see now
who you really are—

a tiny foot bridge,
a hairsbreadth,
a melting pat of butter.

One place to another,
we are all just a
traveling rag-tag band of atoms
seeking light.

Rearview Mirror

I can see how it was,
the slow march of my sadness,
down a well-worn dusty road,
through a dense and suffocating
dark wood.

I thought I was alone.

Now I can see another,
cheering me on
from the edge,
hidden beneath tall cedars,

you there, smiling.

Eventually, I arrive at a place
of warm bread and tea,
laced with milk and cinnamon,
where a brass light with a stained glass shade
bends over a stack of patient,
half-read books.

I am home.

Front Row

Many mornings are mine now.
These familiar days return,
no longer shrouded by sorrow,
a faithful symphony erupts
right on time.

Kingfisher, you are still here,
heron too. Fragrant daphne
near my step, hoods of tulips
and bowing Lenten rose —
how could I have forgotten?

The weeping birch sways
in anticipation and even
the dogwood buds
can no longer contain themselves.

I'm in the front row now,
restless with remembrance —
the opus of an island spring.

Still Life

An Adirondack chair
slung with a worn blue satchel.
A green garden glove, still moist and black,
lies beside a half-empty box of hyacinth bulbs,
abandoned for a cup of tea, a pen,
the blank white page.

In her garden, under the shade
of a sturdy cherry tree,
there is peace.

She turns—
her eyes drawn
to the sound of the front door closing,
tennis shoes springing down wooden steps.

She prays—
as she watches him walk away,
his young shoulders
broadening too fast.

She wonders—
will he ever know
how much his father loved him?

She writes.

Acknowledgments

Many thanks to the editors and journals where these poems have previously appeared, sometimes with different titles or in other versions.

"She Who Shows Up" was first published in *Pulse – Voices from the Heart of Medicine*, September, 2014

"Voyager" was first published in *Wrist Magazine*, volume 8, April, 2013

"Impossible Ledges" was first published in *Poeming Pigeons*, The Poetry Box, 2015

"From the Library of Mussels" was first published in *The Poeming Pigeon: Poems from the Garden*, The Poetry Box, May 2017

"The Morning After You Died" was first published in *Pulse – Voices from the Heart of Medicine*, January, 2018

Praise for *Impossible Ledges*

Dianne Avey's luminous poetic memoir of romance and grief beautifully mixes the images and ambience of island life into a portrait of hearts merging and tearing apart. With excruciating intimacy and precision, she describes "the library of mussels" that mingles memory and sensation into "the opus of an island spring." All lovers of the Pacific Northwest will find fragments of their own heart in Avey's testimony to how her late husband is present in the ebb and flow of life on Anderson Island.

~ Dr. William C. "Liam" Corley,
Professor of American Literature
California State Polytechnic University, Pomona

Impossible Ledges belongs on the shelf with Tennyson's *In Memoriam*. Dianne Avey's poems of grief and consolation are that true and that tender, "small and lovely headstones" that bear "the certain weight of stars." Read them slowly, gratefully, and you will respond with "reverence, / astonishment / and praise" to the gift of her words and the greater gift of life ongoing.

~ Paul J. Willis, author
Deer at Twilight: Poems from the North Cascades

In *Impossible Ledges* by Dianne Avey, we explore illness in the body of poems. Here in this chapbook, poetry becomes memoir and memoir becomes the poems we need to keep close. Poignant and honest, Avey explores loss and the temporariness of this world, "feeling only the certain weight of stars / in an uncertain life." Each tender poem in this love story brings us in and makes us ask, "Where do these remnants go, / the silt of love?" Avey's poems bring us into the moment in beautifully heartbreaking ways.

~ Kelli Russell Agodon,
author of *Hourglass Museum*

Told in the nautical language of an island dweller, these tender poems tell a woman's love story, from first love, marriage, birth of a son, illness and death of her husband, and, finally, her painful emergence into new life. Saturated with the beauty of nature on land and sea, poignant and starkly real, these poems leave you feeling nourished and full."

~ Glenna Cook, author of *Thresholds*
(finalist, Washington State Book Award for poetry)

The lovely nature imagery in Dianne Avey's poems, the tender domestic details and the images of her young son whose father is dying evoke the bittersweet nature of our earthly lives. Avey's journey in poetry is not only one of mourning but is also one that seeks and finds a light that nurtures.

~ Sheila Bender, author
Behind Us the Way Grows Wider: Collected Poems 1980-2013

About the Author

Dianne Avey lives in the Pacific Northwest where she is a fifth generation islander on Anderson Island. She writes poetry where she can, often on the ferry while commuting to her work as a Nurse Practitioner. Her poems and essays have appeared in *Wrist Magazine*, *Pulse*, *The Poeming Pigeon*, *Intima* and several others. For six years, she has organized a successful summer writing retreat on Anderson Island.

Dedicated to her young son, *Impossible Ledges* is a poetry memoir, which tells the chronological true story of love and loss, using her natural seaside surroundings as solace and inspiration.

About The Poetry Box®

The Poetry Box® was founded by Shawn Aveningo Sanders & Robert R. Sanders, who wholeheartedly believe that every day spent with the people you love, doing what you love, is a moment in life worth cherishing. Their boutique press celebrates the talents of their fellow artisans and writers through professional book design and publishing of individual collections, as well as their flagship literary journal, *The Poeming Pigeon*.

Feel free to visit the online bookstore (thePoetryBox.com), where you'll find more titles including:

Keeping It Weird: Poems & Stories of Portland, Oregon

The Way a Woman Knows by Carolyn Martin

Painting the Heart Open by Liz Nakazawa

Epicurean Ecstasy by Cynthia Gallaher

Fireweed by Gudrun Bortman

November Quilt by Penelope Scambly Schott

My Secret Life by Patrick Sheils

The Poet's Curse by Michael Estabrook

Small Blue Harbor by Ahrend Torrey

and more . . .

Printed in the USA
CPSIA information can be obtained
at www.ICGtesting.com
JSHW082057260124
55705JS00008B/113